About this Learning Guide

Shmoop Will Make You a Better Lover*
*of Literature, History, Poetry, Life...

Our lively learning guides are written by experts and educators who want to show your brain a good time. Shmoop writers come primarily from Ph.D. programs at top universities, including Stanford, Harvard, and UC Berkeley.

Want more Shmoop? We cover literature, poetry, bestsellers, music, US history, civics, biographies (and the list keeps growing). Drop by our website to see the latest.

www.shmoop.com

Table of Contents

Introduction

In a Nutshell

Euripides (480-406 B.C.) was a misunderstood genius. His classic *Medea* got totally dissed in its time. It came in third place at the annual Athenian play competition at the Theatre of Dionysus. "Third place," you might say, "that's not tooo too bad." Yeah, except that, as usual, there were only two other playwrights competing. Euripides got trounced by his old rival, Sophocles, and Euphorion, the son of Aeschylus.

Medea's bronze medal probably came as no surprise to Euripides. He is said to be the author of around 92 plays, but he only won the competition five times. Euripides didn't even get to enjoy the final win. The prize (for *The Bacchae*) was awarded after his death. To add insult to injury, Euripides died by being ripped apart by a pack of wild Macedonian dogs. Some scholars say that this story of his death is totally fictional. We hope they're right.

Poor Euripides was always getting picked on. Aristophanes lampooned him mercilessly. The comic playwright made fun of Euripides's use of language and his characters' tendency to spout the new fangled philosophies of Socrates. Like his buddy Socrates, Euripides's ideas were hard for mainstream Athens to swallow. This was due in part to his progressive ideas. The guy was anti-war, sympathetic to slaves and women, and so critical of traditional religion that many believed him to be an atheist. Athens just wasn't ready for these "liberal" ideas.

Euripides was known to be kind of a loner. He spent most of his time writing in a cave on the island of Salamis. Eventually the lack of appreciation and disgust with Athenian politics (especially the destructive Peloponnesian War) may well have been what drove Euripides to leave Athens. He spent the last months of his life in the court of the King of Macedonia, where he proved them all wrong by penning his undisputed classic, *The Bacchae*, and perhaps met a pack of dogs with a taste for playwrights.

In *Poetics*, Aristotle rates Euripides as much a lesser tragedian than Sophocles, pointing out his haphazard plots and un-heroic heroes. These criticisms are valid (both are true in *Medea*), but we wonder if Aristotle ever stopped to think that Euripides had another agenda altogether. While his rival Sophocles was towing the traditional line, Euripides was busy inventing entirely new genres. In retrospect, we can see that it wasn't necessarily that Euripides didn't know how to write a traditional tragedy; he was just dissatisfied with the form altogether.

By blending comic elements with tragic, Euripides basically created Tragicomedy genre. His loosely plotted plays with happy endings created the genre of Romance. And, of course, there's *Medea*, which revolutionized Revenge Tragedies by letting its heroine off the hook. On top of all that, Euripides's focus on the emotional lives of his characters, along with his comparatively natural-sounding dialogue, foreshadowed by thousands of years the creation of modern realism.

History has vindicated Euripides. More of his plays are extant (still around) than any other ancient Greek playwright. *Medea* is now recognized as a timeless classic, while the two plays that beat it in the original competition don't even exist anymore. Euripides is now known as one of the greatest and most innovative playwrights to ever walk the Earth. We're glad the man has finally gotten his due – he was basically a one man dramatic revolution.

Why Should I Care?

Medea's relentless protagonist has become more than just a character. She has become a timeless symbol of feminine revolt. Medea has spent quite some time in male-dominated Greece. As a woman, she has no rights. This is made worse by the fact that she's a foreigner. The people are very suspicious of her because she's way smarter than everybody else. When Medea's husband, Jason, casts her aside for another woman, it's the last straw. Medea responds with violence, even going so far as to kill her own sons.

Some may argue that today's women don't have as much room for complaint as they did back in Ancient Greece. It's undeniably true that the women's rights movements across the world have made incredible progress in recent decades. Of course, there are many countries in the world where women are even worse off than in Medea's day. In some places, women are still bought and sold like cattle and are completely under the thumb of men.

The play's bloody ending is just as shocking today as it was in Ancient Greece. When Medea slaughters her innocent children to get back at her husband, we are forced to question the morality of her actions, as well as those of her male oppressors. Rather than give us a one dimensional, pure-hearted heroine, Euripides gives us a character who is horribly flawed. When Medea gets away with her murderous actions without any repercussion, the play becomes even more disturbing. *Medea*'s complexity and contradictions still spark debate. Its radical message remains just as edgy today as on the day of its first performance.

Summary

Book Summary

At the beginning of the play, Medea's in dire straights. For one, her husband, Jason, has married another woman, Glauke, daughter of Creon the King of Corinth. On top of that, Creon banishes Medea and her two sons from Corinth. Medea, however, is not the kind of woman to take such mistreatment lying down. She swears bloody revenge and swiftly sets about finding a way to kill them all.

First, she convinces Creon to let her stay one more day in Corinth. It goes against his better judgment, but he allows it out of pity for Medea's two sons. This gives Medea enough time to put her plot into motion. Next Medea has to secure a safe place to retreat to once she's committed the murders. By an incredibly lucky coincidence, Aegeus, King of Athens, happens by. Medea promises to cure his sterility if he swears to give her safe harbor. Of course, she neglects to mention she's about to kill a bunch of people.

Now that Medea has the time and a safe place to retreat to, she can really get to work. She snookers Jason into believing that she's now cool with his new marriage. Medea begs her husband to ask Glauke if their two sons can stay in Corinth. Jason is moved and agrees. Medea gives Jason a gossamer gown and a golden crown to sweeten the deal for Glauke. Jason and the children trot off to the palace with hope in their hearts. Their hope is misplaced, however, for once again Medea neglects to mention a vital piece of information: the gifts are cursed.

A Messenger returns and tells Medea all about the horror she has wreaked. When the Princess put on the gown and crown, she received a rather nasty surprise. Her entire body caught fire and the flesh melted from her bones. When Creon saw his daughter's flaming corpse, he was so distraught that he threw his body onto hers and died as well. Medea thinks this is great. Now she only has one thing left to do, in order to leave Jason totally devastated – kill their sons.

The murder of her children isn't easy for Medea. She struggles with her motherly instincts, but in the end her revenge is more important. Medea drags the boys inside the house and kills them with a sword. Jason arrives too late to save his sons. Just as he's banging on the door to stop his wife, Medea erupts into the sky in a chariot drawn by dragons. Jason curses his wife, and she curses him back. He begs to have the children's bodies so that he can bury them. She refuses him even this, and takes their corpses away with her as she flies away triumphant.

Prologue & Parados

- The editor starts by giving us the setting and some back story.
- It is midmorning outside of Jason's house in Corinth.
- Ten years ago, Jason sailed home with his Argonauts, triumphantly baring the Golden Fleece.
- Jason also brought back an Asian bride, Medea.
- Since their return, Jason and Medea have been living happily in Corinth, raising their children.
- Unfortunately, the happy time is over, because Jason has now married a new bride: the daughter of Creon, King of Corinth.
- OK, enough from the editor, on to the play.
- Prologue:
- The old Nurse enters from the house.
- She's having a freak out.
- She laments the fact that the Argo, Jason's ship, was ever built.
- The Nurse cries that she wishes the adventurer had never come for the Golden Fleece, because then her mistress, Medea, would never have helped him get it and would never have fallen in love with the bastard in the process.
- The old lady talks about how Jason and Medea's seemingly perfectly marriage has turned foul. Jason has now married Creon's fresh young daughter.
- According to the Nurse, Medea has been having a major freak out of her own. Ever since she heard of Jason's betrayal she's been inconsolable.
- The Nurse says that her mistress keeps cursing the fact that she ever turned on her own father to help Jason get the Golden Fleece. Medea gave up her home and family for Jason, and now he's gone and dissed her in the worst way possible.

- The grieving Medea apparently now even hates her own sons by Jason.
- The old lady is really afraid that her mistress is going to do something drastic, because Medea is a fierce and vengeful woman.
- A Tutor enters, with Jason and Medea's two sons.
- "What's wrong with you?" the Tutor asks the Nurse.
- The Nurse says she's bummed about Medea's situation.
- The Tutor says that Medea's situation is even worse than she thinks. Creon is planning to give both Medea and her sons the boot.
- The Nurse replies that Jason would never let his sons be treated like that, even if he doesn't like Medea anymore.
- Don't be so sure about that, says the Tutor.
- The Nurse curses Jason, saying he's an enemy to those he's loved.
- "Isn't everybody?" replies the Tutor. He thinks all human beings are only worried about themselves.
- The old lady tells the Tutor to take the kids and keep them away from Medea. She knows her mistress is plotting something and doesn't want the boys to get caught in the crossfire.
- From inside the house, we hear a long tortured moan from Medea. She cries out that she wishes she were dead.
- Fearfully, the Nurse rushes the Tutor and the boys away.
- We hear Medea curse her sons, Jason, and herself. She says that their whole family is doomed.
- The Nurse doesn't understand why Medea is cursing the sons. How is any of this their fault?
- The old lady says that she's glad she's not royalty, because they're often punished for being overreaching.

Parodos (Entry Song)

- The Chorus enters. It's a group of Corinthian women. They're upset about all the drama going on.
- The Nurse agrees that it's a bad situation.
- They hear Medea praying for lightning to strike her.
- The Chorus sings that it's foolish to want to die just because your husband is leaving you.
- Medea cries to Artemis, guardian goddess of women, to bring the palace of Jason's new bride to ruins.
- The Nurse hopes that Medea's grief will soon fade.
- Bring Medea out here, the Chorus says to the Nurse. They want to try and talk some sense into her.

First Episode & First Choral Ode

- Medea finally gets on stage.

- She tells the Chorus that she doesn't want them to think she's snobby for hiding out in the house all day.
- My life has lost all meaning now that Jason has deserted me, says Medea.
- She goes on to observe that women are treated like the lowest form of life on Earth, and lists some reasons why.
- For starters, women's families have to pay huge dowries just to get a man to marry them.
- The women, who rarely have a say in the matter, have to hope against hope that their husband is a nice guy.
- If the husband is a jerk, women are kind of trapped because divorce always makes them look bad instead of the men.
- When men get bored with the marriage, they just go traveling or hang out with their buddies. Women, however, have to stay at home, and are mostly only allowed to talk to their husbands.
- Medea thinks childbirth also stinks. She says she'd rather go into battle any day than give birth.
- Medea tells the Chorus of women, that she has it worse than all of them, because she no longer has a home. She's a foreigner in a strange land and has no one to whom she can turn.
- She begs the Chorus to not stand in the way of her revenge.
- Medea observes that most women are scared of war, but when they're "wronged in love, there is no heart more murderous" (1.76).
- The Leader of the Chorus tells Medea that they won't stand in her way.
- Creon enters.
- The King orders Medea to take her sons and get out of Corinth.
- Medea asks him why she has to go.
- Creon says he's afraid that she'll kill his daughter. Medea has a reputation as a sorceress and Creon thinks she's plotting to use those skills for revenge.
- Medea complains that she's always getting discriminated against because she has a little knowledge.
- She tells Creon that the rumors of her powers are overblown.
- Medea tries to ease the King, by telling him that she's not mad at him or his daughter. She's just angry at Jason.
- Creon doesn't buy it, and tells her again to hit the road.
- Medea pleads with him on her knees.
- The King threatens to have her thrown out forcefully.
- She begs him to let her stay just for the day. There are travel arrangements to be made, and she has to prepare her sons.
- Creon takes a little pity on the sons, and tells Medea that she has until tomorrow to get out of town. If she's still around tomorrow, though, she will be executed.
- Creon exits.
- The concerned Chorus asks Medea what she plans to do now, since she has nowhere to go.
- Medea tells them not to worry, she's got a little something in mind for Jason and his young princess.
- She chastises the Chorus, saying she never would have kissed up to Creon if there wasn't something to gain from it.
- Medea declares that she's going to kill Creon, his daughter, and Jason.

- She ponders how to kill them.
- Should she set their house on fire?
- Perhaps stab the?
- Bad idea, says Medea. She'll get caught if she does those things.
- She decides poison is the way to go.
- Medea realizes that she'd better chill out for a second. If she kills them, no other city will take her in.
- She decides she'd better postpone her revenge until she has some guaranteed shelter.
- Medea swears to use her sorcery to bring them down no matter what.

First Choral Ode

- The Chorus sings a song about the trials of women over the years.
- They observe that women are treated so badly, it's like the universe is askew.
- The women hope that one day their gender will rise to a place of respect that they observe.
- The Chorus empathizes with Medea, who has been jilted out of her home.

Second Episode & Second Choral Ode

Jason enters, quite exasperated.
He lectures Medea that it's all her fault that she and the children got banished. If she hadn't gone around cursing Creon and his daughter, they would've been able to stay in Corinth.
Jason says that he'll give her some money for her impending journey.
She can hate him if she wants, Jason tells her, but he doesn't wish her any harm.
Medea goes off on him, calling him a "criminal" (2.28).
She tells him just how ungrateful he is, pointing out that she saved his life.
Medea says that he never would've gotten the Golden Fleece if it wasn't for her. She helped him with all the tasks required: yoking fire breathing bulls, slaying giant snakes, and tricking the daughters of King Pelias into cutting him up.
She chastises him more, saying that she deserted her father and bore him two sons, yet still Jason betrayed her.
Medea asks her husband where she's supposed to go. She's made half the world her enemy trying to help him.
The jilted woman cries to Zeus, asking him to put outward markings on men indicating just what they're actually made of.
The Chorus Leader observes how terrible it is when love turns to hate.
Jason tells Medea she's exaggerating about how much she contributed to the Golden Fleece adventure.
Anyway, Jason continues, you got way more than you gave. First of all, you now live in Greece, which is way better than the dump in which I found you. Also, you're now famous, and fame is far more valuable than gold.
Medea's husband tells her that he's only marrying the princess out of devotion to his family.

It's not that he doesn't find Medea attractive anymore or that he wants more children at all.
Jason only wants to provide his family with a more stable life by marrying in to royalty.
He chastises his wife for being a silly, jealous woman and not thinking of the greater good of the family.
Jason concludes his speech by observing that, if men could only have kids on their own, they'd have no need of women and the world would be a better place.
The Chorus Leader tells Jason that he had some good points, but that it's just not right to ditch your wife.
Medea tells Jason he should've tried to convince her of some of these points, before he snuck off and took a second wife.
Jason says he didn't think Medea would be into it.
Whatever, says Medea, just admit that you were sick of your aging wife.
Her husband says it had nothing to do with lust. He was only concerned for the happiness of his family.
Medea curses him
Jason gives up and decides to go.
He tells Medea that he'll send her and the children anything they want.
Medea says she doesn't want anything from him.
Jason tells her all her misery is her own fault.
She lashes back, saying he should just go back to his fresh young virgin.

Second Choral Ode

- The Chorus sings of the dangers of love.
- They ask Aphrodite, goddess of love, to never make them lust after someone other than their husbands.
- They also ask that they never be cast out of their homes and country.
- The Leader sings that no man is her friend who would treat their wife as bad a Jason is treating Medea.

Third Episode & Third Choral Ode

- Aegeus enters.
- He greets Medea warmly.
- She asks him where he's coming from.
- He says that he's just come from the oracle at Delphi, where he went to ask Apollo why he can't have children.
- No children, says Medea, aren't you married?
- Yep, Aegeus tells her, but we haven't had any kids yet.
- The Oracle gave him advice that he didn't understand, saying that he shouldn't unstopper his wineskin until he gets back home.
- Aegeus doesn't understand what the prophecy means, so he's swinging through Corinth

on his way to see some dude name Pittheus who knows about this kind of stuff.
- Medea tells him that she hopes everything works out.
- Aegeus asks Medea what's wrong with her.
- She tells him all her woes, and begs him to let her come and stay with him in Athens, promising that she'll use her expertise to help him have children.
- Aegeus is down with this.
- He tells Medea that she has to get to Athens on her own, though. If he took her with him, he would risk pissing off Creon, and that's something he doesn't want to do.
- Medea says that he must swear an oath to protect her when she gets to Athens. She's got a lot of enemies out there, and she wants to make sure Aegeus doesn't sell her out.
- Aegeus agrees and swears on the Earth and the Sun that he'll never drive her from his land.
- Aegeus exits.
- The Chorus Leader wishes Medea a good journey to Athens.
- Medea isn't quite ready to go yet though. Now that she's got somewhere to retreat to, she can carry out her revenge.
- She lays out her plans.
- First, she'll convince Jason that's she's now OK with the marriage.
- Then, she'll beg him to convince Creon to let her sons stay in Corinth.
- Next, she'll send her sons to the princess with some deadly gifts: a gossamer gown and a golden diadem, both doused in poison.
- Then, regretfully, she'll have to kill her own sons.
- After Jason's life and legacy are totally decimated, she'll make her retreat to Athens.
- Medea declares that no man will ever think she's weak.
- The Chorus Leader begs Medea to reconsider her bloody plan, especially the part about killing the boys.
- Medea says there's no use trying to talk her out of it. Killing Jason's sons is way to hurt him the most.
- The Nurse conveniently enters, and Medea asks her to go get Jason.

Third Choral Ode

- The Chorus sings about how blessed and sacred Athens is.
- They ask Medea whether she really thinks such a wonderful place will want a lady who killed her own kids hanging around.
- The Chorus says they don't think Medea is cruel enough to actually kill her sons.

Fourth Episode & Fourth Choral Ode

- Jason enters, with the Nurse.
- He asks Medea what she wants.
- Medea tells him that she's come around to his point of view. She sees now that she was

being ungrateful, for not realizing that he was only trying to help the family.
- She calls for the children and urges them to hug their father. All the strife is over.
- Jason wishes that his sons would hug him like that forever.
- Medea chokes up a bit at loving sight.
- Jason cries a bit, too.
- He praises Medea, telling her he doesn't blame her for acting hysterically before. That's just how women are.
- Medea cries.
- Jason asks her what's wrong.
- She begs him to talk his new wife and Creon into letting the boys stay in Corinth.
- Jason is pretty sure he can get his new wife to agree.
- Medea tells him she'll help out by sending his new wife a gossamer gown and a golden diadem.
- She orders the boys to go inside and bring out the presents.
- Medea says that these items were treasures from her father.
- The boys return with the boxes containing the presents.
- Medea tells them to take the gifts to their stepmother.
- Jason advises Medea not to bother with the gifts, saying he can convince his new wife with no problem.
- Medea argues that gold has stronger bargaining power than anything else.
- She packs Jason and the boys off, telling them to make sure that the new wife touches the items with her own hands.

Fourth Choral Ode

- The Chorus sings of all the terrible things that are about to go down:
- The boys are doomed.
- Jason's new bride is doomed.
- Jason is doomed.
- Medea will have her revenge. (Insert maniacal super-villain laugh here.)

Fifth Episode & Fifth Choral Ode

- The Tutor enters with the boys and tells Medea the good news: the princess has agreed to let the boys stay in Corinth.
- Medea emits a wail of pain.
- The Tutor doesn't get what she's so sad about; he thought he was bringing good news.
- Medea tells him not to worry about it.
- She hugs the boys close to her and laments the fact that she won't see them grow up.
- Suddenly, Medea has a change of heart, telling the Chorus that she'll take the boys away with her instead of killing them.
- She changes her minds again, saying they must die.

- Medea goes back and forth a couple more times and finally decides that murdering her sons is necessary.
- She says that she knows she's doing evil, but that her passionate desire for revenge is stronger than her will.

Fifth Choral Ode

- The Chorus sings about the perils of parenthood.
- They talk about how wearying it is raising a child and how people without offspring are happier overall.
- They end by recognizing how terrible it is when a full grown child dies and question whether the joys of parenting are worth the potential for grief.

Sixth Episode & Sixth Choral Ode

- A Messenger runs in.
- Panicked, he tells Medea to run. The Princess and Creon are both dead.
- Medea is tickled pink and asks the Messenger to tell her every grisly detail
- The Messenger launches into the story:
- He talks about how excited all the servants were when the boys showed up. They were all glad that there was peace between Medea and Jason.
- At first, the princess was all snobby towards them, but then Jason talked her into letting the boys stay.
- Medea's presents sealed the deal.
- Jason and the children left the house, thinking everything was cool.
- The Princess was all about the gifts. She put the gown and diadem on and pranced around the palace looking at herself in the mirror.
- Then things got ugly.
- Her skin changed color, her eyeballs bulged, and she started foaming at the mouth.
- The princess shrieked in pain.
- The diadem caught fire and the gossamer gown ate away her flesh.
- Her whole body caught fire and clots of blood dripped from her.
- She ran around until she finally collapsed with pain.
- Her flesh dripped from her bones.
- Then Creon showed up.
- The King was stricken with grief and grabbed his daughter's flaming body. He caught fire too, and, before you knew it, his flesh was also bubbling from his bones.
- Before too long two ghastly corpses were lying on the palace floor.
- The Messenger tells Medea that she'd best have a good escape route.
- Before taking his leave he observes that there's no such thing as a happy human being.
- The Chorus Leader says she feels bad for the princess.
- Now Medea says that it's time to kill her sons. She tells herself that they'd be killed

anyway after the assassination. It's better that it be by her hand.
- Media pushes down her feelings of motherly love and enters the house to murder them.

Sixth Choral Ode

- The Chorus prays to the Sun and the Earth to stop the murders.
- They ask if there was any point in the boys being born at all and observe that people who kill their own family will be haunted forever.

Seventh Episode & Envoi

- The boys are heard desperately shouting for their lives inside the house.
- They go silent.
- The Chorus members lament Medea's heinous actions, and tell a story of another woman who killed her own sons by jumping off a cliff with them in her arms.
- Jason shows up. He's furious.
- He asks the Chorus where Medea is. Not that it matters, though, he says, because there's nowhere she can hide after killing Creon and his daughter.
- Jason says he's worried what Medea might do to their sons.
- The Chorus agrees that he should be worried. They tell him to open the doors to the house.
- Jason draws his sword and beats of the doors, trying to open them.
- A great rumbling is heard.
- Medea appears in the sky with the boys' corpses beside her.
- She's in a chariot drawn by dragons. (Really, she is.)
- Medea says her grandfather, the Sun, (yes, the actual Sun) gave her the dragon chariot to protect her from enemies.
- Jason heaps curses on Medea.
- He shouts that a Greek wife never would've been so cruel. He should've known better than to marry a foreigner.
- Medea tells him he can say whatever he likes. She's won, by hurting him to the core.
- Jason yells that she's hurt herself, too, by killing her own sons.
- She retorts that it was worth it and tells Jason that the whole thing is his fault, because he married another woman.
- Jason replies that her crime is far worse, and that he knows the children will live on in Medea's guilty mind.
- Medea says, enough of you. I'm going to take off on my dragon chariot now.
- Jason begs her to leave him the boys' bodies so that he can bury them.
- Nope, says Medea, I'm going to place their bodies in a temple to Hera, where no one will violate the bodies.
- Medea adds that she's going to start a festival in Corinth in honor of the boys.
- She tells Jason that she's off to Athens now, where she'll find sanctuary.

- Jason pleads to touch his children's flesh one last time.
- Medea refuses.
- Jason curses Medea a couple more times and cries that he wishes his children had never been born.
- Medea flies away.

Envoi

- The Chorus concludes the play by recognizing how unpredictable the will of the gods is.

Themes

Theme of Women and Femininity

Medea sharply criticizes the male-dominated society of its time. Its protagonist is a radical anti-heroine who continues to inspire both admiration and fear. We sympathize with Medea's downtrodden state and applaud her strength and intelligence. However, her bloody and vengeful rebellion shocks and unsettles audiences even to this day. The play can be seen as a cautionary tale to oppressors as well as the oppressed.

Questions About Women and Femininity

1. How can Medea be seen as symbol of feminine revolt?
2. What are the major complaints Medea raises about the treatment of women?
3. What hierarchy exists among the women in *Medea*?
4. Is *Medea* still pertinent to the issues facing women today?

Chew on Women and Femininity

Medea is symbolic of the intelligent woman caged by patriarchy.

Theme of Revenge

Medea's relentless pursuit of vengeance is legendary. She is driven by a passionate desire to right the wrongs done to her and sacrifices even her own children in the pursuit of satisfaction. *Medea* shows audiences the horror that can come when a person lets desire for revenge rule her life. Euripides's play helped pave the way for many later revenge tragedies, from the numerous Spanish revenge dramas to Shakespeare's *Hamlet*.

Questions About Revenge

1. Why does Medea think it's necessary to kill her sons to get revenge on Jason?
2. How do you interpret the fact that Medea suffers no consequences for her revenge?
3. What steps must Medea take in order to achieve her revenge?
4. What's the difference between revenge and justice?

Chew on Revenge

Medea is a cautionary tale on the horrors that revenge can cause.

Medea's lust for revenge makes her an unsympathetic character.

Theme of Betrayal

All the violence and terror in *Medea* is caused by Jason's betrayal of his wife Medea. Her sheer rage at his unfaithfulness drives her to commit horrific acts of bloody revenge. Ironically, Medea's fury at her husband's betrayal drives her to the use of trickery and manipulation, which are really just another form of betrayal. *Medea* shows how, when one person betrays another, all may be corrupted.

Questions About Betrayal

1. In what ways can Medea's manipulations be seen as betrayal?
2. Does Jason's betrayal justify Medea's revenge?
3. Is Jason's second marriage really a betrayal at all? Why or why not?
4. Could Medea's murder of her children be interpreted as a betrayal?

Chew on Betrayal

Jason's unfaithful behavior and lack of sensitivity towards Medea is symbolic of the overall unfair treatment of women.

Jason never betrayed his family or Medea; he only acted in their best interest by marrying Glauke.

Theme of Exile

Medea is laced throughout with the theme of exile. All the characters relate to the motif. Some, like Medea, have been banished from their homes; some are the ones doing the banishing. The theme of exile would have resonated strongly with Euripides's audience of ancient Athenians. Their city-state was their lives. The thought of being cut off from it and cast out into the wilderness would have been terrifying.

Questions About Exile

1. In what ways does Medea bring her banishment on herself?
2. How is Medea in some ways responsible for Jason's exile from his home town of Iolcus?
3. Is it wrong of Creon to banish Medea? Why or why not?
4. How does Medea's exile from her homeland heighten the stakes surrounding her banishment?

Chew on Exile

Jason's betrayal of Medea is worsened by the fact that she forsook her father and homeland for love of him.

Medea's banishment is her own fault, as her threats of Creon and his daughter are what cause it.

Theme of Foreignness and 'The Other'

Ancient Greeks had a deep suspicion of foreigners, thinking of them all as "barbarians." With *Medea*, Euripides seems to confront this prejudice by choosing to honor a foreigner with the role of tragic heroine and by making her the most intelligent character in the play. However, the playwright also confirms many Greek stereotypes of foreigners by making Medea wild, overly passionate, and vengeful.

Questions About Foreignness and 'The Other'

1. Does *Medea* confirm or refute Greek prejudices toward foreigners?
2. In what ways is Medea prejudiced against Greeks?
3. How do Medea's foreign origins affect her social status?
4. How can Medea be seen as a "typical Asian" in the eyes of the Greeks?

Chew on Foreignness and 'The Other'

Medea defies Greek conceptions of uncultured foreigners by making its heroine the most intelligent character in the play.

Medea confirms Greek notions of barbarous foreigners by depicting its heroine as violent and vengeful.

Theme of Marriage

Medea is an extreme depiction of just how bad a marriage can go. It really doesn't get much worse than the marriage seen in this play. When Jason takes a new wife, Medea, his former wife takes revenge by killing four people, including their two sons. Indeed, the play doesn't exactly have a bright outlook on matrimony. In *Medea* the severing of a marriage releases the same destructive force as the sundered atom of a nuclear bomb.

Questions About Marriage

1. How were ancient Greek ideas of marriage different from modern concepts? How are they similar?
2. What overall view of marriage does the play seem to take?
3. Was Jason's second marriage truly a betrayal? Why or why not?
4. What power dynamic was present in ancient Greek marriages?

Chew on Marriage

Medea can be interpreted as a searing indictment of the institution of marriage.

Euripides's two divorces are perhaps reflected in his cynical portrayal of marriage.

Theme of Cunning and Cleverness

Medea is symbolic of the clever woman imprisoned in a world of men. Her intelligence inspires both suspicion and cautious admiration. In the end, her cunning becomes her supreme weapon in her quest for revenge. None of her enemies stand a chance against her supreme intellect. *Medea* shows that, without a doubt, the greatest power lies in knowledge.

Questions About Cunning and Cleverness

1. What tactics does Medea use to manipulate those around her?
2. How does Medea's intelligence make her dangerous?
3. In what ways does Medea's superior intelligence ostracize her?
4. How does Medea put her cunning to use in the play?

Chew on Cunning and Cleverness

The community's mistrust of Medea is heightened by the fact she's smarter than everybody else.

By depicting a foreigner as being smarter than all the Greek characters, Euripides defies Greek prejudice against foreigners.

Theme of Love

Aphrodite, Goddess of Love, is not very well appreciated in Euripides's *Medea*. Everywhere her hand is seen, destruction swiftly follows. Whether the love be romantic, paternal, or maternal, it always leads to death and despair. Quite often the characters even go so far as to beg the goddess to spare them the pains that love can bring. Overall, *Medea* seems to present a rather cynical view of the tenderest of emotions.

Questions About Love

1. How does romantic love affect the action of the play?
2. Do you think Jason ever loved Medea? Why or why not?
3. What overall view of love does the play seem to take?
4. In what ways does each character express paternal or maternal love?

Chew on Love

Love is a force of destruction in *Medea*.

Creon's sympathy towards Medea's sons, along with his love for his daughter, make him quite a sympathetic character.

Quotes

Women and Femininity Quotes

Medea: Of all creatures that can feel and think,
we women are the worst treated things alive. (31)

Thought: Euripides boldly states the central theme of the play: the sorry state of the female in Greece. This theme popped up in many of his plays. He is noted for taking up the cause of women as well as the next lowest group on the totem pole: slaves.

Medea: we [women] bid the highest price in dowries
just to buy some man
to be dictator of our bodies [...]
How that compounds the wrong! (31)

Thought: This isn't necessarily accurate, as girls' fathers paid dowries. Still, though, Medea's outrage is more than justified. Women were basically bought and sold like cattle. Though they were above slaves on the social ladder, they were at times still treated like nothing more than property.

Medea: Divorce is a disgrace
(at least for women),
to repudiate the man, not possible. (31)

Thought: Women were in some ways prisoners. If they got sold off to a man who mistreated them, there was really no good escape route. The rest of society would reject them if they left their husband.

Medea: I had rather stand my ground three times among
the shields
than face a childbirth once. (31)

Thought: Is Medea by some standards a "masculine" woman? Here she says she'd rather do battle than give birth. In some ways, this is a rejection of the foundation of the traditional role of women.

Medea: Well, suppose they are dead: [...]
will any man afford me home in a country safe
for living [...]? (57)

Thought: Even a woman as powerful as Medea feels the need to be protected by a man. You'd think that she be all right on her own. She does have a couple of dragons at her disposal. The fact that she still wants a man around, even after her last one dissed her so badly, seems to show just how deeply entrenched patriarchy was in Greek society.

Chorus: One day the story will change:
then shall the glory
of women resound [...]
Reversing at last the sad
reputation of ladies. (58)

Thought: The Chorus seems to be almost sounding a battle cry for a feminist revolution. We wonder how this would've been received by the all-male audience that attended the plays in ancient Athens. Of course, it would've been performed by male actors as well.

Chorus: If only Apollo,
Prince of the lyric, had put
in our hearts the invention
Of music and songs for the lyre
Wouldn't I then have raised
up a feminine paean
To answer the epic of men? (58)

Thought: The Chorus is pointing out that their culture's depictions of women have all been created by men. This idea, that their entire culture is male centered, wouldn't pop up again until the twentieth century. *Medea* was in many ways ahead of its time.

Chorus: Woman of stone, heart of iron,
Disconsolate woman, ready to kill
The seed of your hands with the hand that
tilled. (193)

Thought: Is the play damaging to women in some way? It's definitely revolutionary in its blatantly pro-woman themes. We have to question, though: if you're trying to champion the feminine cause, why make your heroine a serial killer? Aristophanes, Euripides's comic contemporary, would later satirize *Medea* for that very reason.

Jason: Oh, I married a tigress,
not a woman, not a wife,
and yoked myself to a hater and destroyer (204)

Thought: Could it be argued that Jason and the patriarchal (male-run) society that he represents turned Medea into this monster? Perhaps the lack of respect for her in part drove her to her horrendous actions.

Jason: You think it right to murder
just for a thwarted bed.
Medea: And do you think that a thwarted bed
is trifling to a woman? (212-213)

Thought: In Greek society women mostly only had power through their husbands. The loss of his bed would've been bad news.

Revenge Quotes

Nurse: [Medea] hates her sons [...] I dread to think of what is hatching in her mind. (1)

Thought: Euripides doesn't shy away from some pretty obvious foreshadowing here. Medea's path of revenge is pretty clear even from the opening moments of the play. Of course, the Athenian audience the play was written for would've already know the Medea myth quite well.

Medea: Oh, what misery! [...] Cursed sons, and a mother for cursing! Death take you all – you and your father [...]
Nurse: Why make the sons share in their father's guilt? (20-21)

Thought: The Nurse points out the irrationality of Medea's rage. This lady is so out of control that she plots to annihilate all products of she and Jason's union. The boys' innocence is no defense against the irate Medea

*Medea: [Creon] lets me stay one extra day, to make three enemies corpses:
ha! father, daughter, and my husband. (57)*

Thought: There's an incongruity here. Medea does end up killing Creon and his daughter, but doesn't make any attempt to kill Jason. Also, she makes no mention here that she plans to kill her sons. It's unclear if she just changes her mind somewhere along the way, or if she's lying about her exact plans. Of course, it could also be sloppy plot-making on the part of Euripides.

*Jason: Anything you or the children want in exile,
let me know; I'll gladly furnish it [...]
Medea: The presents of the wicked are pure poison. (58)*

Thought: Jason seems to feel guilty about the way everything is going down. By denying his help in exile, Medea keeps him from easing his conscience. It's yet another way that she gets revenge on her husband.

*Leader: But, my lady, to kill your own two
sons [...]?
Medea: It is the supreme way to hurt my husband. (140-141)*

Thought: Medea's hatred for Jason is so fierce that she'll go to any lengths to hurt him. She feels that her revenge wouldn't be complete if the boys are left to live. By the end of the play, Jason is destroyed.

*Jason: But, Medea, what is this --
these dewy eyes, these tears; [...]
Medea: It is nothing.
I was just thinking of our sons. (150-151)*

Thought: It's open to interpretation as to exactly why Medea is crying here. They could be fake tears, meant to convince Jason of her sincerity. She could also be lamenting the fact that she's going to murder her sons in a very short period of time.

*Medea: how I bless you both [...]
not here—beyond [...]
every blessing here you father has despoiled. (173)*

Thought: Some scholars claim that this is Medea's best argument for the murder of her sons. They represent her marriage, which has been tainted by Jason. Therefore, they must be destroyed.

Medea: My heart dissolves
When I gaze into their [her son's] bright irises [...]
Why damage them in trying to hurt their
father,
and only hurt myself twice over? (173)

Thought: Here Medea seems to sincerely waver in her resolve. She is touched by the closeness of her sons. This softer moment reveals a tender side of the character, which is often overlooked.

Messenger: A king's home a charnel house –
and you rejoice? [...]

Thought: Medea seems to sincerely enjoy all the gruesome details of that the messenger relates. Her revenge satisfies her greatly. She differs from most tragic protagonists because she doesn't end up regretting her actions. Ultimately, she's OK with how everything turns out.

Jason: Murder is punished, and you'll be destroyed
by the avenging phantoms of you children. (224)

Thought: If *Medea* were like most Greek tragedies, Jason would be right about this. However, Medea, gets off scot free. Nobody takes out any revenge on her and, though she shows some regret about murdering her children earlier in the play, she doesn't seem all that bummed out as flies away on her dragon chariot.

Betrayal Quotes

Nurse: Jason has betrayed his sons and [Medea], takes to bed a royal bride. (22-23)

Thought: This is the inciting incident of the play. Jason's betrayal of Medea's bed causes all of the horrific things that follow. How much accountability does he have in the deaths at the end of the play?

Medea: Woman, on the whole, is a timid thing:
[...] but, wronged in love,
there is no heart more murderous. (31)

Thought: Jason's betrayal has unleashed a primal rage in Medea. Here she suggests that all women get just as vengeful when wronged by their man. Though there are many *Jerry Springer* episodes to support this statement, it seems like a bit of a stereotype to us.

Medea: I can unload some venom from my heart
and you can smart to hear it.
To begin at the beginning, [...]
I saved your life (60)

Thought: Medea's rage at Jason's betrayal is deepened by the fact that she's done so much for him. If it wasn't for her, he never would've gotten the Golden Fleece and would never have achieved epic hero status. Ironically, it's this status that made him a worthy mate for Creon's daughter.

Jason: were you [Medea] living at the world's ends,
your name would not be known. [...]
Oh, to me, houses crammed with gold, [...]
are nothing with no name. (62)

Thought: Jason seems to think that his having made Medea famous somehow makes his betrayal OK. However, Medea never demonstrates the same need for fame that Jason finds so valuable. This weakens his argument greatly

Jason: I wanted above all
to let us live in comfort, not be poor (62)

Thought: Jason doesn't seem to see his actions as a betrayal at all. He contends that the only reason he married Creon's daughter, was to provide his family, including Medea, with a better life. This is probably his most credible argument, though the idea is alien to most modern audiences.

Medea: Go, my sons, into the halls of wealth;
down on your knees and beg her –
this new wife of our father's (161)

Thought: Medea could be seen as a traitor as well. She's purposely involving her sons in a plot which will make everybody in Corinth want to kill them. You might say that her betrayal is far worse than Jason's.

Medea: My heart dissolves
When I gaze into their [her son's] bright irises [...]
Why damage them in trying to hurt their
father,
and only hurt myself twice over? (173)

Thought: Besides betraying her sons, might Medea also be betraying her self in some way? Though she's doesn't seem too upset about killing her sons, she does a good bit of crying about it beforehand. You could look at it like her destructive side is betraying the gentler side of her nature.

Medea: What power or divine one is ready to hear you [Jason]:
perjurer, liar, treacherous guest? (225)

Thought: Medea feels that the gods are on her side. In her mind, she's only bringing justice to the situation. Jason betrayed her and he deserves what he gets. The play seems to support this idea. Medea receives no divine punishment for her actions. In fact, she gets away on a chariot once given to her by her grandfather Helios, the sun god.

Jason: I'd rather they'd never been born to me
Than have lived to see you destroy them this
day. (238)

Thought: To the end, Jason is completely unrepentant of his betrayal. Notice that he doesn't say he wishes he'd never taken another wife. Instead he says that he wishes his children had never been born.

Chorus: Wide is the range of Zeus on Olympus,
Wide the surprise which the gods can bring (239)

Thought: Euripides is often thought to have been an atheist. There is some debate about this, but it's pretty hard to deny that he often depicts gods as uncaring or cruel. If Zeus allowed all these things to happen, could that be interpreted as a betrayal? Or has man betrayed him by doing all these terrible things?

Exile Quotes

Nurse: [Medea] might be a rock or wave or the sea, for all she heeds of sympathy from friends, except sometimes to […] moan to herself about her father--whom she loved--and her country and the home she sacrificed (1)

Thought: Medea gave up everything to help Jason in his quest for the Golden Fleece. She made herself an exile out of love for Jason. Ironically, his betrayal has made her an exile once more.

Nurse: She never would have baited Pelias' daughters
to the murder of their father. (1)

Thought: Pelias was the king of Iolcus and Jason's uncle. Medea tricked his daughters into chopping him up, hoping to help Jason gain the throne. The people of the city didn't take it so well and chased Medea and Jason from the city. In effect, both Medea and Jason have been exiles the entire time they've lived in Corinth

Nurse: Ah, she [Medea] has merited this city's good opinion,
exile though she came (1)

Thought: It says a lot that Corinth previously thought well of Medea. Especially after the mischief she got up to in Iolcus. We wonder what exactly made the Corinthians accept her. Maybe, it was all her smarts and skills. Probably, though, they just accepted her because Jason was a famous hero, and it was widely known that she was instrumental in his quest.

Medea: O Father, my country, the land I abandoned,
Flagrantly killing my brother (26)

Thought: The violence of Medea's exit from her homeland has made her a permanent exile. This fact heightens the stakes of the entire play. Medea is backed into a corner with nowhere to turn, making her all the more dangerous.

Creon: Go, Medea. Remove yourself.
Get packing from this land. […]
it is reported that you threaten me […]
and of course the bride and groom. (35)

Thought: It's hard to deny that Creon has a pretty good reason for kicking Medea out of Corinth. What else is he supposed to do? She's going around saying that she's going to kill everybody.

Medea: Well, suppose they are dead:
will any city take me in, […]
and shield me from reprisals? (57)

Thought: Medea has to find another city-state to retreat to, after she commits the murders. This will help protect her from the inevitable retribution from Corinth, but there's more to it than that. To the ancient Greeks, their city-states were there worlds. The thought of roaming the land without a civilized place to call home was horrifying.

Jason: I should like you to remain.
But you, Madam,
obstinate in folly,
have continuously reviled our royalty,

And so you are banished. (59)

Thought: Jason blames Medea for her exile from Corinth. Is his argument in anyway credible? Yeah, she has been going around threatening the royal family, which isn't the best move. It seems, however, that Jason would've been able to predict such a reaction from his spouse. It's likely that he would've known exactly how Medea would react, when he took another wife.

Jason: When I came here from the land of Iolcus, [...]
I, a wretched fugitive (59)

Thought: It's important to note that Jason is an exile as well. He's originally from Iolcus, not Corinth. He's actually heir to the throne of Iolcus, but was exiled from the city after he and Medea conspired to have King Pelias, Jason's uncle, killed by his daughters. Jason's desperate desire to regain royal status undoubtedly motivates his marriage to Creon's daughter.

Chorus: Death: I would bargain with death,
To die such a day to a finish.
For nothing is like the sorrow [...]
Of losing your native land. (80)

Thought: Here the Chorus expresses the depth to which ancient Greeks felt an affinity towards their native city. Many Athenians would've have totally agreed with the sentiment that death is better than exile.

Medea: I have no father, home, defense from danger.
Oh, the mistake I made was when I left his house (137)

Thought: Often in the play, Medea expresses deep regret at having made herself an exile. She seems especially regretful about severing ties from her father. This distance from her dad is, perhaps, the worst exile she's had to endure.

Foreignness and 'The Other' Quotes

Nurse: Ah, she [Medea] has merited this city's good opinion,
exile though she came (1)

Thought: Medea was accepted into Corinthian society when she first showed up. She was treated like any Greek woman. Now that her husband has dumped her, however, she's treated as a foreigner. The Greeks are very suspicious of her because she's a foreigner.

*Nurse: her [Medea's] home she sacrificed
to journey here
with a man – oh – who disdains her now. (1)*

Thought: Medea betrayed her father to help Jason capture the Golden Fleece. Doing so was a great sacrifice. She doomed herself to forever being a foreigner at a time in history when being foreign could be a very dangerous thing.

Nurse: Yes, now [Medea] knows at a terrible first hand what it is to miss one's native land. (1)

Thought: Though Medea has lived in Corinth for a while, she is still seen as an outsider. The fact that she has a Greek husband and has given him sons does little to stem the prejudice against her. Could this distrust on the part of the Greeks contribute to her rage?

*Nurse: she glares with a bull-mad glaze
(Or is it a lioness with her whelps)
When anyone comes or speaks of helps. (29)*

Thought: Greeks were of the opinion that all Asians, like Medea, were wild and emotional, especially the Persians, who they'd once defeated in war. Comments like this reflect this stereotype. It's almost like the Nurse is saying, "Well, you know how those people are."

*Medea: I agree, of course,
that a foreigner should conform,
adapt to his society (31)*

Thought: Medea recognizes her status as an outsider and concedes that she ought to act more Greek. Of course, her extreme grief and need for revenge doesn't seem particularly un-Greek to us. There's a ton of other tragedies that show Greeks behaving just as badly.

*Medea: I am alone, […]
uprooted from a foreign land. […]
So, please, I ask you [Chorus] this:
if I can find a way to pay my husband back –
your silence. (31)*

Thought: Here Medea uses her status as a foreigner to appeal to the Chorus. She plays on their sympathies, by emphasizing how isolated she is. It works pretty well, too. Medea manages to convince these Corinthian women to stand idly by while she assassinates their royal family.

Jason: So [...] this is not the first time
I have seen irrevocable damage done
by a barbarous rage. (59)

Thought: When Jason uses the word "barbarous" he's making a direct reference to the fact that Medea is not Greek. The word comes from the Greek *barbaros* which simply means foreign. Now, of course, the word is associated with wild and unruly behavior. It's highly likely that the modern connotations come directly from Greek prejudice towards outsiders. With the line above, Jason seems to be blaming Medea's fury on the fact that she's a foreigner. (59)

Jason: you [Medea] have a home in Hellas [Greece]
instead of some barbarian land.
You have known justice (62)

Thought: Jason is under the impression that Medea should be grateful for the time she's spent in with him in Greece. He views himself as having rescued her from a dark and savage land. There would've most likely been some Athenians in the audience who agreed with Jason on this front. We wonder, however, if Euripides is trying to show his audience that they might be just a little bit full of themselves. After all, Medea is by far the most intelligent person in the play. She moves all the "enlightened" Greeks around her as easily as chess pieces. Would a stupid barbarian be able to do this?

Medea: Oh, the mistake I made was [...]
trusting the word of a man from Greece (137)

Thought: Medea is showing some prejudice of her own here. She seems to imply that all Greeks are just as untrustworthy as Jason. Medea, like all tragic heroines, is definitely not free from flaws.

Jason: At last I understand
what I never understood before,
when I took you from your foreign home to live
in Greece, [...]
No woman in the whole of Hellas [Greece]
would have dared so much (204)

Thought: Jason again reveals his Greek prejudice to outsiders with this statement. Of course, it's pretty understandable, since Medea has just slaughtered four people, including her own children. It's probably safe to say that the play didn't go a long way toward changing Athenians' opinions of foreigners.

Marriage Quotes

Nurse: [Medea] was in everything Jason's perfect foil, being in marriage that saving thing: a wife who does not go against her man. (1)

Thought: These lines reflect the ancient Greek idea that in a healthy marriage, men had all the control. As long as women behaved and did what they were told, everything was cool. Euripides's *Medea* could be seen as a cautionary tale, warning its Athenian audience of the dangers of such an imbalance of marital power.

Tutor: The father does not love his sons, but –
his new wedding bed. (16)

Thought: Check it out: Medea isn't the only one who thinks Jason's second marriage is messed up. Even the slaves think it's not a nice move. Of course, the Tutor's whole position in life is threatened by the new marriage. If Medea and the boys get exiled, what will happen to him?

Chorus: your husband has gone to adore
A new bride in his bed, why, this
Has often happened before. (25)

Thought: The Chorus begins the play by trying to talk some sense into Medea. You shouldn't be freaking out so much, they say. It's not like Medea is the first person to get dumped. Over the course of the play, however, Medea seems to win the Chorus over to her side.

Chorus: Deep is her sobbing from depths of pain:
Shrill the news her suffering brings
Of marriage betrayed (30)

Thought: Jason rips a hole in Medea's soul when he takes another wife. The severing of her marriage creates an unholy rage in Medea. You'd think he'd know better than to mess with her after the bloody deeds he's already witnessed her do.

Jason: I should like you to remain.
But you, Madam,
obstinate in folly,
have continuously reviled our royalty,
And so you are banished. (59)

Thought: Jason's claim here that he was hoping that Medea would stay, even though he'd taken a new wife, isn't as crazy as it sounds. It was totally respectable for a Greek man to have a wife and a concubine. Today, he seems like a total jerk, but to an Athenian audience his argument would've been a lot more credible.

Medea: I even bore you [Jason] sons [...]
just to be discarded for a new bride.
Had you been childless,
this craving for another bedmate
might have been forgiven. (60)

Thought: Part of a woman's perceived duty in marriage was to provide her husband with sons. Medea feels extra cheated because she fulfilled her end of the bargain. Jason has what many men, like Aegeus, crave, yet he throws it all away.

Medea: What a charming record for our new
bridegroom this:
"His own sons and the wife who saved him
are wayside beggars." (60)

Thought: Medea seems to have a good point here. If Jason would ditch his current family to gain social status, isn't he likely to do something similar in the future? This theory never gets a chance to be tested, of course, because Medea kills his new wife.

Medea: Aegeus, I beg you, [...]
by these knees I clasp, [...]
let me come to Athens, shelter me,
accept me in your home. (123)

Thought: In some myths, Medea went on to marry Aegeus once she got to Athens, evidently giving *his* wife the boot. Medea eventually gave Aegeus a son named Medus, though there was some speculation as to whether Medus was really the son of Jason. Once again though, Medea gets kicked out of a Greek city. When Aegeus' long-lost illegitimate son Theseus shows up, Medea tries to poison him. Aegeus figures out who Theseus is just in time and Medea is kicked out of Athens.

Jason: I did not blame you [Medea]
It is natural for a woman to be enraged
when her husband goes off making second
marriages. (150)

Thought: Jason's statement shows that he's not totally devoid of sympathy. After Medea tricks him into thinking that she's sorry for her behavior, he concedes that maybe he was a little insensitive. It's too little too late, for Medea, who relentlessly proceeds with her revenge.

Medea: For I must go in exile to another land:
never have my joy in you,
or see your bright young progress;
never deck your brides, your marriage bed,
or light you radiant to your wedding day. (173)

Thought: Medea becomes moved when she imagines the boys' nonexistent futures. It's interesting that she focuses on marriage here, since hers has turned out so badly. Could she be longing in a way for the purity of love that her marriage once had?

Cunning and Cleverness Quotes

Nurse: Ruthless is the temper of royalty: [...]
How much better to live among equals. [...]
Let me decline in a safe old age.
The very name of the "middle way" (21)

Thought: Wise words. You could argue that the Nurse's simplistic logic makes her the smartest cookie on stage. Euripides was not only famous for taking up the cause of women but slaves as well. With his dignified portrayal of the Nurse, he's doing both at the same time.

Creon: You [Medea] are a woman of some knowledge,
versed in many an unsavory skill. (35)

Thought: This is one of the first recognitions in the play that Medea is a skilled woman. Her knowledge of drugs and witchcraft give her power. This makes everybody around her nervous, especially since she has a bit of a temper.

Medea: Because I have a little knowledge,
some are filled with jealousy,
others think me secretive, and crazy. (36)

Thought: Here Medea says that she's discriminated against just because she's smart. This is undoubtedly true. Of course, she certainly doesn't help eliminate these prejudices when she uses her skills and cleverness to murder four people.

Medea: In point of fact, my knowledge
does not amount to much. (36)

Thought: Medea plays down her knowledge in an attempt to seem less threatening to Creon. The king, however, doesn't buy this argument at first. Medea's skills are well known, as is her cunning.

Creon: You are dangerous.
All your cleverness
shall not keep you here. (37)

Thought: It's amazing that Creon is so aware of Medea's craftiness yet he still allows her to stay in Athens for a day. This could be seen as some rather dubious plotting on the part of Euripides. His plays have often been accused of having sub-par plots, causing some scholars to place him below his contemporary, Sophocles.

Medea: Plot, Medea, devise you recipes:
advance to the deadly act that tests your
courage. (57)

Thought: Much like modern superheroes, tragic heroes and heroines are usually extraordinary in some way. Medea's "super power" is her intelligence and skills at witchcraft. When she is threatened, she turns to these abilities for protection.

Medea: you are a born woman:
feeble when it comes to the sublime,
marvelously inventive over crime. (57)

Thought: It's interesting that the word "crime" is used here. The word seems like a bit out of a contradiction as Medea says elsewhere that her devilish plan is just. Perhaps, we're to view Medea's actions as both just and unjust at the same time. This kind of paradox is typical of many tragedies.

Medea: Swear by every god and godhead. [...]
Never yourself to drive me from your land,
and if an enemy of mine tries to drag me off,
never while you live to let go.
Aegeus: I swear by the Earth and sacred light of the Sun (132-133)

Thought: Medea's cunning is on full display when she makes Aegeus swear this oath. She knows that the Corinthians will hunt her no matter where she goes after she takes her revenge. Aegeus would never consent to harboring her if he knew what she planned. Now, however, he is bound by the gods to protect her no matter what.

Medea: Now I can unfold to you [Chorus] my whole design:
there is nothing sweet in it, as you will see (137)

Thought: Medea unveils her crafty plan to the Chorus, reminding us very much of a comic book super villain. The strategy of revealing one's diabolical scheme seems dubious. Doesn't it make it a lot easier for the hero to unravel the plan? Indeed, it never works out for Dr. Octopus. Spiderman always foils his wicked plots. Of course, Medea is the heroine of this play, not the villain, and her cunning scheme goes off without a hitch.

Medea: Jason please forgive me for all the things I
said. [...]
I have been out of my mind, hysterical. [...]
Jason: I praise you now,
Medea,
and I did not blame you (150)

Thought: Medea is apparently the cleverest person in Corinth. She's easily able to manipulate Jason into believing that she's no longer mad at him, even though she's ranting and raving for days. It's sort of amazing that he falls for this so easily. The play would have a lot more dramatic tension if Medea had at least one worthy adversary.

Love Quotes

Nurse: My mistress, Medea, then would never have [...] been struck to the heart with love of Jason. (1)

Thought: It's important to remember that the root of all Medea's anger is love. She fell for Jason hard back in their Golden Fleece days. This deep affection is the fuel for her almost inhuman need for revenge.

Nurse: Oh, what an enemy [Jason's] proved to those he should have loved!
Tutor: What human being is not? (15-16)

Thought: The Tutor here expresses a pretty cynical view of love. The play seems to back this theory of humanity. Everyone from Jason to Medea act only with themselves in mind.

Medea: Love, did you say?
It is a mighty curse. (44)

Thought: Love is often depicted as a force of destruction in Euripides's plays. Frequently his characters' passion is the cause of their undoing. *Hippolytus* is another play where this occurs. In that piece Phaedra falls in love with her stepson, Hippolytus, and tragedy ensues.

Leader: How frightening is resentment
how difficult to cure,
When lovers hurl past love
at one another's hate. (61)

Thought: Here again we see love depicted as the seed for the worst kind of hatred. Jason and Medea's venom for each other is so intense, because their love was just as passionate.

Jason: Well, as far as I'm concerned
it was Aphrodite and no one else in heaven or earth
who save me on my voyage, [...]
it was [...] sheer shooting passion,
that drove you [Medea] to save my life. (62)

Thought: This seems like a pretty flimsy argument to us. Why does the fact that Medea helped Jason out of love negate the fact that she helped him? What does Jason think would be a better motivation for Medea's assistance? Power? Personal gain? Jason, it seems like you're just digging yourself a deeper hole.

Chorus: Love is a dangerous thing: [...]
But, oh, if the goddess should visit
A love that is modest and right,
No god is so exquisite. (80)

Thought: Here again we have a very cynical view of love. The Chorus seems to be saying a healthy relationship is impossible. From the perspective of the play all love inevitably leads to tragedy.

Medea: So sweet [...] the mere touch of you:
the bloom of children's skin--so soft [...]
their breath--a perfect balm. (173)

Thought: This is one of the few places in the play where we see that Medea is capable of real maternal love. This sweet moment is goes a long way towards humanizing Medea. It shows that even though she is capable monstrous actions, she is also capable of gentle affection.

Messenger: But her father, [Creon] unawares, poor man,
rushed headlong through the room,
flung himself lamenting on the body,
hugged and kissed it, sobbing out: [...]
"O god's [...] let me die with my daughter." (182)

Thought: The Messenger relates to us one of the most touching (and grotesque) scenes in the play. Creon shows true paternal love when he discovers his daughter's body. He's so overcome with emotion he doesn't stop to think that maybe it's a bad idea to throw yourself onto a flaming corpse. Once again in the play we see love as a destroyer.

Medea: My own hands shall them, they shall be
carried
to the sanctuary of Hera on the Cape,
where no enemy shall ever do them harm of violate their sepulchre.
Here in Corinth, [...]
I shall inaugurate a solemn festival (233)

Thought: Medea's intention to honor her dead sons seems to show that her maternal love is still intact somewhere inside her. Of course, a couple questions come to mind. 1) Wouldn't it have been a greater honor not kill them in the first place? 2) How is Medea going to start a festival in Corinth, when she can never go back there again?

Jason: Dearest children!
Medea: Dear to their mother.
Jason: And so she slew them.
Medea: To get at your heart.
Jason: You did! You did! How I long to press
my little children's lips to mine! (230-234)

Thought: In the end, Medea sacrifices her love for the sake of revenge. Unlike most tragic protagonists she seems to feel all right with her decisions. Once again this seems to support the view that the play has a very cynical view of love. Medea is a lot happier and self satisfied now that she's completely destroyed all traces of it from her life.

Plot Analysis

Classic Plot Analysis

Initial Situation
Medea mourns Jason's betrayal.
At the start of the play, Medea is a mess. Her husband, Jason, has married King Creon's royal daughter. Medea's slaves, the Nurse and the Tutor, worry about what terrible things their mistress might do in retaliation.

Conflict
Medea gets banished and swears revenge.

Creon shows up and tells Medea that she and her two sons are banished. Medea's been talking too much trash about the marriage, and the King is afraid she might do something drastic, like kill everybody. Our heroine pulls on Creon's heartstrings and convinces him to let her stay one more day. As soon as the King is out of earshot, Medea swears to murder him and his daughter.

Complication
Aegeus promises protection, which allows Medea to continue her revenge plot.
Medea tricks Aegeus, King of Athens, into offering her sanctuary. Now she has somewhere to run after she does her killings. She manipulates Jason and her sons into taking the Princess some cursed gifts. As a result, both Creon and his daughter are burned alive by magic flame.

Climax
Medea kills her sons.
After savoring all the gory details of the royal family's incineration, Medea proceeds to the final, and most painful, step in her plan. In order to wound Jason as deeply as she possibly can, she takes their two sons inside and kills them with a sword.

Suspense
Jason batters doors.
Jason shows up too late to save his sons. He batters on the door of the house trying to get inside. Before he can get in, Medea erupts into the sky in her private dragon chariot. She mocks Jason from the sky with her two boys' corpses beside her.

Denouement
Jason and Medea have one last debate.
Medea and Jason have their last bitter shouting match. They both blame each other for what has happened. Jason begs to bury his sons or at least to touch them one last time. Medea refuses.

Conclusion
Medea escapes. Jason is devastated.
Medea flies ways in her dragon drawn chariot. Her revenge is complete. Her husband is emotionally destroyed.

Booker's Seven Basic Plots Analysis: Tragedy

Anticipation
Medea plots bloody revenge.
Medea, like many tragic heroes and heroines, starts off with single minded determination. No matter what it takes, she's going to make Jason pay for taking another wife. Medea determines to kill the girl and her royal father Creon. There are also strong hints that Medea is plotting to kill her and Jason's two sons.

Dream Stage

Aegeus offers sanctuary.
The only hitch in Medea's plan is that she needs a safe place to hide after she does murder. Incredibly conveniently, Aegeus, King of Athens, shows up. Medea promises to solve his sterility if he'll give her sanctuary. He agrees, and the stage is set for assassination.

Frustration Stage
Medea tricks Jason.
Medea manipulates Jason into thinking that she's OK with his new marriage now. She begs him to convince his new wife to let her sons stay in Corinth. This is, of course, all a ploy to get a couple poisoned gifts into the hands of the unfortunate Princess. Jason offers a little resistance to taking the gifts, but not too much. Ultimately, the frustration stage isn't that frustrating for Medea.

Nightmare Stage
Medea kills Creon and his daughter.
Things get ugly. The Princess and Creon go up in flames as a result of Medea's cursed gifts. The description of their deaths is pretty nightmarish to say the least. Meanwhile, Medea goes through some emotional turmoil about killing her sons.

Destruction or Death Wish Stage
Medea kills her sons and flies away.
Medea commits the horrible act of infanticide, killing her two sons. Unlike most tragic figures, she suffers no repercussions for her actions. She flies away in her dragon-drawn chariot, without having to pay for her crimes. Jason tells her that she'll be haunted with guilt, but she seems to think she did the right thing. Euripides boldly defies traditional tragic structure by letting his heroine get away unscathed.

Three Act Plot Analysis

Act I
Medea is in the depths of despair, because her husband, Jason, has married a new wife, the daughter of Creon, King of Corinth. The news only gets worse when Creon shows up to tell Medea that she and her two sons are banished. At the end of this act, Medea decides to quit moping and get pro-active about her situation. Her solution? Bloody revenge. She manipulates Creon into letting her and her sons stay another day, so she'll have enough time to carry out her vindictive schemes.

Act II
Medea has to do a little maneuvering to pull off her plan. First she convinces the unwitting Aegeus, King of Athens, to harbor her. Then she tricks Jason into thinking that she's cool with his new marriage now. She asks him to talk his new sweetie pie into letting Medea's kids stay in Corinth. To help with the convincing, Medea offers some lovely gifts. Or should we say...lovely, poisoned gifts. Jason, who must've forgotten that Medea is a crafty sorceress, agrees, and he and the kids take the gifts to the palace. Act II peaks as the Messenger brings news that Creon and his daughter have been incinerated by Medea's cursed gifts.

Act III
There's just one step left for Medea to have total revenge on Jason: she must kill their sons. She feels it's the way she can wound him the deepest. She hems and haws a bit, wrestling with her maternal instincts, but in the end her lust for vengeance wins. The play climaxes as our heroine takes her two sons into the house and executes them. Act III concludes with Jason and the unrepentant Medea trading a few last bitter words, before Medea makes a get away on her flying dragon chariot.

Study Questions

1. Is there ever a just reason for murder?
2. In what ways does a play like *Medea* help the cause of women? How might it hurt it?
3. Compare the plight of women Euripides day to today's society. Similarities? Differences?
4. Directors often set Greek tragedies in another place and time other than Ancient Greece. If you were directing, where and when would you choose? Why?
5. What would the play be like if it had been written from the perspective of a different protagonist? Jason? Creon? The Nurse?

Characters

All Characters

Medea Character Analysis

Medea is a straight up serial killer. Let's take a look at her bloody career. Back in her and Jason's Golden Fleece days, she killed her own brother and chopped him into pieces. Later on, she tricked King Pelias' daughters into chopping him into pieces. During Euripides's play, she incinerates King Creon and his daughter, Glauke. She concludes this bloody rampage by slaughtering her own two sons. Medea, what in the name of Zeus is wrong with you?

Though Medea is a highly intelligent woman, she lets passion rule her actions. When her husband, Jason, marries Glauke, Medea goes totally nuts. This, of course, is understandable. When your husband takes another wife without telling you, you definitely have the right to be more than a little angry. Of course, burning the flesh from the bones of his new bride is an extreme reaction. Add to that the assassination of her amiable father, and Medea's actions appear even more drastic. When you top all that off with the killing of she and Jason's innocent sons, Medea, the underdog, becomes nearly impossible to root for.

We should point out that Medea is not a total monster. Though she revels in the gruesome deaths of Creon and Glauke, she shows a good amount of motherly affection towards her two boys. This is shown when she says things to them like, "So sweet [...] the mere touch of you: the bloom of children's skin – so soft [...] their breath – a perfect balm" (173). She wrestles with herself before she finally decides to kill them. This emotional conflict creates in Medea the kind of psychologically complex character for which Euripides is celebrated.

Medea's rage also goes beyond anger at Jason's betrayal. She's mad at the whole of society. She's definitely has it bad. 1) She's a foreigner, making the people of Corinth distrust her. 2) She's a woman, so she has next to no rights in the male-dominated Greek society. 3) She's an intelligent woman, which makes the men even more uncomfortable. When Jason takes a new wife and Creon banishes her, Medea's plight becomes symbolic of the struggles of all women. Therefore, her violent reaction becomes a form of radical political resistance. With his Medea, Euripides created one of Western literature's most archetypal symbols of feminine revolt.

Medea Timeline and Summary

- Medea laments the fact that her husband has taken a new wife.
- She wins the Chorus over to her side by appealing to them as fellow woman and then declares revenge.
- She convinces Creon to let her and her sons stay in Corinth one more day, then secures safe harbor with King Aegeus of Athens.
- Next, Medea tricks Jason into thinking that she's cool with his new marriage.
- She manipulates her husband into asking Glauke if her kids can stay in Corinth.
- Once this is done, she sends Jason and the boys off with cursed gifts for Glauke.
- Still, Medea vacillates as to whether she should kill her sons.
- She decides the boys' death is necessary and then revels in the news that Glauke and Creon have been incinerated.
- She slaughters her two boys.
- Then, she erupts into the sky in a dragon-drawn chariot.
- She trades some last bitter words with Jason.
- Medea flies into the night, taking with her the bodies of her sons.

Jason Character Analysis

Jason is kind of a jerk. If you took him on *Oprah*, he'd get a stern talking to. After years of marriage with Medea, he goes and marries somebody else: Glauke, daughter of Creon. When Medea gets mad about it, he acts like she's just being an overemotional woman, saying "You women are all the same" (62). He goes on to say, "What we poor males really need is a way of having babies on our own – no females, please. Then the world would be completely trouble free" (62).

By placing these choice sexist remarks in the mouth of Jason, Euripides creates a character who is symbolic of the intensely patriarchal Greek society. As is mentioned in Medea's "Character Analysis," this makes Medea's revenge against him larger than just the actions of a jealous woman. When Medea decimates Jason with her bloody actions, it's as if all chauvinistic males have been dealt a lethal blow.

Jason's insensitivity knows no bounds. Without the help of Medea's cunning and magic, Jason never would've gotten the Golden Fleece. He wouldn't be a legendary hero at all. Ironically, he wouldn't even be considered worthy of Creon's royal daughter. When Medea points out how much he owes her, he callously downplays her contribution, saying, "Your cleverness played a part" and "your service did no harm" (62). How does this guy take himself seriously? It boggles the mind that he could say this to a woman who gave up her family and homeland for the love of him.

His insensitivity is further shown when he tells Medea she should be grateful for having had the chance to live in Greece at all. He says to her, "You have a home in Hellas [Greece] instead of some barbarian land" (62). So, Medea is supposed to grateful to her noble Greek husband for having rescued her from her crude homeland? Medea was a princess of the wealthy kingdom of Colchis. She is the granddaughter of the Sun. We highly doubt she was living in a mud hut. Comments like this make Jason symbolic of Greek xenophobia (fear of foreigners) as well. Such prejudice against foreigners was widespread in Greek society.

OK, enough Jason bashing. He does have one justification for his second marriage which is almost credible. He tells Medea that "I was not [...] tired of your attractions [...] it was simply that I wanted above all to let us live in comfort, not be poor" (62). It was perfectly respectable for a Greek male to have more than one family. By marrying Glauke, Jason rescues both himself and Medea from poverty, and assures their sons a place in society. He never planned on Medea being banished; she would have stayed on as his concubine. He points out that she brought the banishment on herself by going on about how she was going to kill Creon and his daughter. This is true. Though this justification is hard for a modern audience to swallow, it would've made sense to ancient Athenians. Of course, the very fact that this sort of arrangement was commonplace speaks to the overall sexism of Greek society that Jason represents.

Jason Timeline and Summary

- Jason chastises Medea for overacting about his new wife.
- He tries to justify his actions, saying that he wanted to rescue his family from poverty.
- Then Medea manipulates him into asking Glauke to let his sons stay in Corinth.
- Along with his sons, Jason unknowingly delivers Medea's cursed gifts.
- He rushes home to save his sons from Medea, but is aghast as Medea launches into the sky, bearing the corpses of their sons.
- Jason curses Medea over and over again and begs her to let him bury the bodies, but is denied.

* He curses Medea one last time as she flies away.

Chorus Character Analysis

There has been some serious scholarly smack talk concerning Euripides's use of choruses. The main criticism is their lack of effect on the action of the play. The Chorus in *Medea* is a good example of this. This group of Corinthian women mostly just hangs out, bemoaning the terrible things that are going down. The only time we see them actually try and do something is at the beginning of the play when they attempt to lift Medea from her melancholy. They advise:

If your husband has gone to adore
A new bride in his bed, why, this
Has often happened before.
Do not harrow your soul. For Zeus
Will succor your cause. What use
To lessen your life with grief
For a lost lord? (25)

The Chorus's arguments have no effect on Medea. In fact, our crafty protagonist ends up pulling the Corinthian ladies to her side, by appealing to them as fellow women imprisoned in a world of men. By the time Medea's done with them, they're singing an ode of female revolution. The ladies intone:

Back to their fountains
the sacred rivers are falling;
The cosmos and all morality
turning to chaos.
The mind of a man is nothing but a fraud
[...]
One day the story will change:
then shall the glory
or women resound,
And reverence will come to the race of woman,
Reversing at last the sad reputation of ladies. (58)

For the rest of the play the Chorus does nothing to stop Medea's bloody deeds. Some point this out as sloppy plotting of Euripides's part. It's odd that these women stand idly by as Medea, a foreigner, plots to assassinate their royal family. Creon seems like a nice enough guy. Yeah, he banishes Medea, but she was going around threatening to assassinate him and his daughter. It even turns out that he's an old softy, when he allows Medea to stay another day for the sake of her sons. So why would the Chorus do nothing to stop the murder of their amiable ruler?

The only justification we can come up with for the Chorus's inactivity is that, like Medea, they are extremely dissatisfied with the treatment of women in their society. Their ode to female revolution supports this idea. Perhaps they represent the large number of women that are put upon, but don't have the will for revolt. They could be seen as living vicariously through Medea. Perhaps she serves as an outlet for their repressed rage. Of course, even the Chorus balks when Medea takes it as far as killing her own kids. The Corinthian women pray fervently for Zeus to stop her. Unfortunately, their prayers go unanswered, and once again they are unable to affect the action of the play.

Rather than using the Chorus to advance or complicate the plot, Euripides chooses to use them to expound upon his themes. This is true in many of his plays. In *Medea* they sing of the destructive power of love, the sorrows of exile, and the horror of Medea's murderous revenge. They also serve to release the tension between each episode. Euripides's unconventional use of the Chorus is yet another example how he challenged the dramatic status quo of his day. Over the course of his career they became less and less essential to his dramas. Some scholars theorize that, if he'd had his way, he would have fazed them out altogether, instead filling the plays with more of the realistic dialogue which he is so famous for inventing. In the Athenian dramatic competitions, however, this unconventional step would have been sacrilege.

Chorus Timeline and Summary

- The members of the Chorus try to talk some sense into Medea.
- After listening to her, though, they sing an ode to feminine revolution and lament Medea's banishment.
- They also sing on the destructive power of love.
- Later, they chant about what a great and enlightened place Athens is and wonder if Athens will accept a murderess like Medea.
- They bemoan the upcoming murders and observe that parents are worse off than people who don't have kids.
- The Chorus members pray to the Zeus to stop Medea from killing her sons.
- They conclude the play by observing that Zeus works in mysterious ways.

Character Roles

Protagonist

Medea

Unsurprisingly, Medea is the protagonist of *Medea*. Her relentless pursuit of vengeance against Jason is the central spine of the play. Medea is the perfect protagonist in many ways, because she causes everything to happen. She tricks Creon into giving her another day in Corinth – time enough to hatch her scheme. She manipulates Jason and her sons into taking poisoned gifts to Creon and his daughter. She murders her children.

The character is a great example of the fact that not all protagonists have to be "good guys." Indeed, a character like her would be a villain in a lot of plays. She's a vengeful, child-murderer. However, in dramatic analysis nobility has nothing to do with whether a character is the protagonist or not. The most important factor is who drives the action. In this light, it's hard to deny that Medea emerges at the end of the play as its blood-spattered but undisputed protagonist.

Antagonist

Jason

Jason is a classic antagonist. He does Medea wrong and she sets out to bring him down. He's definitely weak as antagonists go. It's doubtful that an audience would ever think he's going to get the better of Medea.

Even in their first debate about whether or not his second marriage was justified, Jason's rationalizations come off as pretty flimsy. Medea's verbal retorts make mince meat of him. Later on, the crafty Medea skillfully manipulates him helping to take her cursed gifts to his new wife, without even breaking a sweat. You'd think Jason might know his wife a little better than to trust her so blindly. But, nope…the bumbling Jason plays right into her hands.

The conclusion of the play might be one of the rare times that an audience sympathizes more for the antagonist than the protagonist. Sure it wasn't very cool for him to take a new wife. Sure he's insensitive about the whole thing. But Medea takes it too far by killing their children. Even if the audience doesn't feel bad for the disloyal Jason, chances are they might just see more sense in his final argument than Medea's.

Character Clues

Actions

As in most drama, the characters of *Medea* are mainly defined through their actions. Medea's vengeful nature is revealed in her plotting and murdering. Jason's ultimate disloyalty is shown when he kicks his wife to the curb for fresh young virgin. Creon shows that he's an old softy when he lets Medea stay another day on account of her sons. And, of course, there's the dutiful Nurse, whose sense of loyalty overrides her own morality as she stays true to her mistress, Medea, throughout bloody events of the play.

Social Status

Social status plays an important role in defining the characters in *Medea*. First, there's the Nurse and the Tutor who, being slaves, are the lowest on the totem pole. They have to just do what they're told no matter what.

Medea is a foreigner which makes her have the next lowest status. Even though she is of royal blood, it's of an Asian kingdom, so that doesn't count with the Greeks. And of course, she's a woman, which doesn't give her a lot of power in Ancient Greece. Medea's low social status adds fuel to her anger, and helps to fan the flames of revenge.

Let's also consider Jason's social status. He's a legendary hero, so he's got a certain amount of clout. Also, though, he's a man of royal blood that's never had the chance to rule. This undoubtedly fuels his desire to marry Creon's daughter, which of course is what starts all this terrible business to begin with.

Family Life
You can learn a lot about the characters in *Medea* by the way they treat their family. Both Jason and Medea express love for their sons, showing that each of them has a softer side. Of course, this is kind of negated when Jason deserts them and Medea kills them. The true family man of the play seems to be Creon, who dies when he throws himself on the flaming corpse of his beloved daughter.

Literary Devices

Symbols, Imagery, Allegory

The Sons
Medea's killing of her children is symbolic in several ways. First, the boys are a pretty clear representation of Medea and Jason's marriage, as they are the product of what was once a loving relationship. Medea feels like Jason has betrayed and soiled that marriage by taking a new wife, so she's out to destroy every last remnant of it. It's surprising she doesn't burn down the house, too. Instead, Medea satisfies herself with slaughtering her kids in the house where they were born, sacrificing them on the altar of revenge.

As we mentioned in "What's Up With the Ending? ", the murder of the sons could also be a symbolic act of feminine revolt. Medea is put upon by the male-dominated society around her – banished by Creon, deserted by her husband. She could be seen as rebelling against the role of mother, in which women were often trapped. There's nothing wrong with being a mother; the problem comes when that's all you're allowed to be. Also, it's probably no coincidence that Medea's final act of revolution is to kill two young boys. You could interpret the murder as the destruction of the next generation of potential oppressors. In the end, the slaughter of Medea's sons seems to be a symbolic act of bloody resistance.

Gods and Goddesses
Divine entities are often used in Greek drama for symbolic purposes. Indeed, the gods themselves are said to have been symbols of natural or emotional forces that were beyond human comprehension. Using the name of a god or a goddess would have brought up very specific meanings for the Athenian audience. In *Medea*, Euripides, like his contemporaries, invokes the names of the gods often. Let's take a second to analyze a few of Euripides's shout-outs to the gods:

Helios
First there's Helios, the Sun god. In the translation we used, by Paul Roche, Helios is mostly referred to simply as the Sun. He was said to have ridden his shining golden chariot (the sun)

across the sky each day. Helios is probably the most significant god in the play. He's Medea's grandfather. Helios was a Titan, one of the older and more primitive gods, which were later replaced by more "civilized" beings. Medea's "barbaric" behavior could be seen as a result of her relation to this volatile and primal force of nature.

The Sun god is also the only divine presence to directly affect the action of the play.Several of the gifts Helios has given his granddaughter are used in key plot points. The golden diadem and gossamer gown which Medea gives to Creon's daughter were both originally from Helios. When the gown and crown shoot out flames, it's like the Sun itself is attacking the Princess. The dragon-drawn chariot that serves as Medea's get-away car is also a gift from her grandfather. When Medea flies away in this junior version of Helios's flaming chariot, it's as if the Sun god has symbolically sanctioned her vengeful actions.

Apollo

Apollo was the god of many things, including reason, poetry, the arts, and prophecy. Like Helios, he was also a Sun god. Apollo was part of the second generation of gods who, led by Zeus, replaced the Titans. What's interesting is that Apollo never totally replaced Helios in the Greek imagination. They existed side by side as gods of the Sun. (We wonder if they ever argued over who got to drive the flaming chariot that day.)

By using the names of both Sun gods, Euripides seems to symbolize the basic conflict at the heart of the play: Greek reason vs. "barbarian" passion. To the Greek Jason it's perfectly rational that he marry Glauke. It gives his family, including Medea and her children, wealth, power, and security. Medea's wild passion doesn't allow her to accept this rationale. To her, it's much more basic. She just sees her husband marrying some other woman and responds with "barbaric" violence.

This idea of Apollo being on Jason's side is strengthened when the Chorus basically accuses the god of chauvinism. They sing:

The ballads of ages gone by
that harped on the falseness
Of women, will cease to be sung [...]
If only Apollo,
Prince of the lyric, had put
in our hearts the inventions
Of music and songs for the lyre
Wouldn't I then have raised
up a feminine paean
to answer the epic of men? (58)

The Chorus asks Apollo why he hasn't blessed any women with the art of poetry. If he had, then perhaps the depictions of women in Greek tradition would have been a great deal more sympathetic. This is, of course, a pretty ironic thing for a male playwright to have his characters say, especially since his female protagonist is notoriously unsympathetic. Still, this passage helps support the theory that the Apollo of *Medea* is firmly on the side of men and is symbolic of Jason's side of the argument.

Hecate

It's no surprise that Medea, a symbol herself of feminine revolt, mostly prays to goddesses rather than gods. Besides, Helios, her grandfather, she prefers to gain strength from the female side of the pantheon. Most important of all to Medea is Hecate, who Medea describes as "the goddess who abides in the shrine of my inner hearth – the one I revere most of all the gods" (57). Hecate is a lot like Artemis, who Medea also calls upon. Both goddesses represent nature and are virgins. Both are potent symbols of girl-power, making them ideal figures for Medea to call upon.

Hecate, however, is a much older goddess than Artemis. Like Medea's grandfather Helios, Hecate was a Titan. In some mythologies she is said to have helped Zeus overthrow her fellow Titans. It's interesting that, once again, Euripides shows Medea favoring the older, more primal deities, ones that might be cooler with her "barbaric" ways.

Like Medea, Hecate was also a foreigner. The Greeks created many conflicting mythologies about her as they tried to weave her into their pantheon. Hecate's cult is thought to have originated somewhere around modern day Turkey, which is the same area that Medea is said to have been from. The fact that Medea and Hecate originated from the same general area ties them even closer together.

By Euripides's time, Hecate had come to be associated with witchcraft. Though her name didn't have this connotation when she first showed up in Greece, to this day she is thought of as a goddess of witches. She's even been appropriated by modern Wiccans and Neo-Pagans. Once again this connection with witchcraft makes her a good fit for Medea, who has mad sorcery skills of her own.

In some mythologies, Hecate was seen as an avenger of women. When Medea calls on the goddess to bless her revenge, she symbolically summons the energy of all women ever done wrong by men. In a way this elevates Medea's bloody deeds above the level of petty revenge.

Though she is mentioned only once by name, Hecate is alluded to a couple of other times. The Chorus tells the story of the Trojan Queen Hekabe who, like Medea, killed her children. In some myths Hekabe became Hecate's dog after she threw herself into the sea. Also, Jason insults Medea by saying she's like the Tuscan Scylla, a sea monster that some said was the child of Hecate.

Setting

Corinth, Greece, in front of Jason and Medea's house

Medea is set in a city-state called Corinth. It's interesting that, though most Greek tragedians lived in Athens, their plays are hardly ever set there. In fact, they weren't allowed to do so. Guess it just hit to close to home. The tragedies did almost always examine issues that Athens was currently wrestling with. However, Athenians seemed to have preferred a little objective distance when thinking about their problems.

Athenians also seemed to dig objective distance in terms of time. Tragedies were almost always set back in the day, somewhere in Greece's distant mythical past. Euripides and his fellow tragedians drew from their culture's rich tradition of heroes and gods to weave their tales. Jason and Medea are great examples of this.

More specifically, the play is set in front of Jason and Medea's house. This seems quite appropriate. It's a tragedy that shows the bloody dissolution of a family. What better place to set the play than in front of the house in which the family once thrived? It's ironic that this place that once gave them shelter is now the setting for mutually assured destruction.

Genre

Drama, Tragedy

We say the play is a drama because, well, you know...it's a play, a piece of literature that can only be fully appreciated when presented before a live audience. More specifically we dub it a tragedy. Of course, Euripides was a famous rule breaker and genre bender, so *Medea* has some big differences from most other Greek tragedies. The most significant of these is that Medea's *hamartia* doesn't cause her undoing.

The *hamartia* is most often called a tragic flaw, but the word is more accurately translated as a "mistake in judgment." A hero or heroine's *hamartia* typically causes their undoing. Usually they die, or mutilate themselves, or are at least driven insane with guilt. None of these things happen to Medea, however.

It's like Euripides sets his audience up for the expected downfall, then whisks the carpet out from under their feet right at the end. Medea definitely seems to have a *hamartia*. It's certainly a mistake in judgment to murder four people, including your own children, just because you got dumped. You could definitely say that Medea's passionate vengefulness is a character flaw. However, in the end, it's everybody else that suffers, not Medea.

Tone

Cynical, Sympathetic

Overall, *Medea* doesn't exactly paint a pretty picture of humanity. For one, its two main characters don't have too much in the way of positive qualities. Jason forsakes his wife, Medea. Medea kills their children. Neither one of these people could be said to be particularly sympathetic. On top of that, neither one learns anything by the end of the play. By the conclusion, they're both still convinced that they've each done the right thing, and that the other is to blame.

The play also seems to take a pretty cynical view of love. Over and over again, love is a force of destruction not joy. Medea and Jason's relationship began with love, and, well, we all know the marriage didn't turn out particularly well. Even Creon's poignant display of love for his daughter causes his destruction; he throws himself on her flaming corpse, and he too is consumed.

Of course, the play is not without sympathy. Most of this comes through the Chorus. They express a great deal of sympathy for Medea's plight at the beginning of the play. Beyond that, Euripides seems to use them as a mouthpiece for his views on the mistreatment of women in Athenian society. The Chorus, along with every other character, also expresses sympathy for Medea and Jason's poor doomed children.

Writing Style

Polemical, Modern Precursor

Medea is an unabashed polemic, meaning that Euripides has some pretty specific opinions and he wasn't afraid to talk about it. The play is still, to this day, one of the most radical texts of feminine revolt in all of Western literature. The first thing Medea does when she goes on stage is list, in extensive detail, all the reasons why it stinks to be a woman. This was a pet theme of Euripides and can be found in many of his plays. *Medea*, however, stands out as the most uncompromising.

Euripides is also widely considered to be the most "modern" of the ancient tragedians. Evidence of this can be seen in *Medea*. Yeah, it still uses a chorus, verse, and heightened language, but in comparison to some of the other plays of its time, the play's dialogue sounds quite natural. The characters speak in a much closer approximation of everyday speech than in the plays of Aeschylus and Sophocles.

Euripides is known for having been the first Greek playwright to start exploring the psychologies of characters. This is also a pretty modern concept. Medea is a powerhouse role that's been taken on by many great actresses over the years. The character's emotional pyrotechnics give a lot for an actress to sink her teeth into.

While Euripides's focus on character was often at the expense of a solid plot, it made him really popular with actors. Some scholars believe that is why more of his plays made it through the ages than any other Greek playwright. Actors may have kept the plays around so they could show off their stuff.

What's Up With the Title?

After extensive research, including the consultation of eminent scholars and the examining of ancient texts, we are prepared to declare, once and for all, the meaning of the title. It's a play about Medea, so Euripides called it *Medea*.

What's Up With the Ending?

The ending of *Medea* has caused debate for thousands of years. It's chock full of contradictions and conundrums. For one, it defies the conventions of tragedy by letting its protagonist off the hook. Medea commits four murders, the most horrendous being the slaughter of her own children. Instead of making his heroine pay for her crimes, Euripides saves her using a *deus ex machina*. The term translates to "god from the machine" and has come to be used anytime a playwright resolves their play with a sudden surprise ending. Medea's escape in the dragon chariot given to her by the god Helios is a classic example of *deus ex machina*. Euripides is infamous for such endings and has been criticized greatly for them. Why, oh why did you do it Euripides? What are we to make of Medea's escape?

It's doubtful that an audience is supposed agree with Medea when she says she only did what was right. Sure Jason did Medea wrong, but is killing their kids really the appropriate response? Even Medea recognizes this when she says, "Why damage them in trying to hurt their father?" (173). In the end, though, revenge is more important to Medea than maternal love, and she kills her children in order "To get at [Jason's] heart" (233). Her methods are effective; Jason is decimated at the end of the play. It's highly unlikely that the majority of audience members, modern or ancient, would think the jealous slaughter of innocent children is good.

So, if we're not suppose to condone Medea's monstrous actions, what exactly are we supposed to take from all this? Is there a moral to this story?

Some scholars think that Euripides's great sympathy towards women is the reason he lets Medea fly away. Medea's violence is the result of oppression. She's put upon by a male dominated society and cast aside like old baggage by her husband. When faced with this incredibly unfair treatment, Medea responds with a shocking act of bloody resistance. By killing her children, she's rebelling against the dominant role of women in her time: motherhood. Also, notice that the children she kills are both males. In a way, she's stopping another generation of potential oppressors from gaining power. The fact that she gets away with it, makes the ending even more unsettling. It's almost as if Euripides wanted to leave his all-male Athenian audience with a note of warning – beware those you oppress. One day they might not take it anymore, and you may not be able to do anything about it.

Did You Know?

Trivia

- Euripides was divorced twice, once because his wife cheated on him. (Source)
- *The Cyclops*, by Euripides is the only extant (still in existence) satyr play. (Source)
- According to legend, Euripides was born on the same day of Athens' famous defeat of the Persian Empire. (Source)
- After news reached Athens of Euripides's death, Sophocles honored his rival at the next dramatic competition by dressing his chorus in black robes. (Source)

Steaminess Rating

PG

There's no sex in *Medea*. Our heroine does spend a good amount of time chewing out her unfaithful husband, Jason, for lusting after his new virgin wife. The unfortunate Jason doesn't get much of a chance for lust, however, when Medea murders the girl. In *Medea*, sexual frustration plays a much bigger role than sex itself.

Allusions and Cultural References

Literature and Philosophy References

- Argo, the ship that Jason sailed on when he went to get the Golden Fleece (1, 59, 204)
- Pelias (1, 59)
- Themis (26, 27, 30)
- Artemis (26)
- Zeus (27, 30, 46, 193, 205)
- Hecate (57)
- Sisyphus (57)
- Helios (57)
- Apollo (58, 84, 91)
- Aphrodite (62)
- Orpheus (62)
- Cypris (80)
- Harmonia (144)
- Maids of Pieria (144)
- Furies (185)
- Tuscan Scylla (204)
- Hera (193, 223)

Best of the Web

Websites

Aristotle
http://www2.cnr.edu/home/bmcmanus/poetics.html

This page provides a good overview of Aristotle's thoughts on tragedy. It's interesting to consider how *Medea* fits and also breaks Aristotle's definition of a tragedy.

Euripides's Biography
http://www.theatrehistory.com/ancient/euripides001.html
A great bio on Euripides from TheatreHistory.com.

Movie or TV Productions

Medea, 2005
http://www.imdb.com/title/tt0441581/
A modernized version for TV.

Medea, 1988
http://www.imdb.com/title/tt0095607/
Directed for TV by revolutionary director Lars von Trier.

Medea (1983)
http://www.imdb.com/title/tt0213875/
A TV version starring the famous Zoe Caldwell.

Medea, 1969
http://www.imdb.com/title/tt0066065/
Starring opera star Maria Callas.

Historical Documents

Full Text of the Play
http://records.viu.ca/~johnstoi/euripides/medea.htm
Here's a link to a translation of the play. It's not the one we used, but it may be interesting to compare.

Aristotle's *Poetics*
http://classics.mit.edu/Aristotle/poetics.html
Read what Aristotle had to say about tragedy.

Video

Judith Anderson
http://www.youtube.com/watch?v=6rG_yAhX0PM
Check out Judith Anderson as Medea.

Zoe Caldwell
http://www.youtube.com/watch?v=zlnoTXKyOvI
Here's Zoe Caldwell in the title role.

Maria Callas
http://www.youtube.com/view_play_list?p=A2D37A1E85EAA17F&search_query=medea+maria+callas

The opera star plays the tortured Medea. The full movie is available on YouTube in 12 parts.

Images

A Classic Portrait
http://www.utexas.edu/courses/larrymyth/images/medea/AB-Medea-Sandys.jpg
Here's a famous painting of Medea.

A Modern Interpretation
http://www.safran-arts.com/art/misc-Medea.jpg
Check out this creepy modern painting of Medea.

A Recent Revival
http://entertainment.timesonline.co.uk/multimedia/archive/00298/medea-385_298856a.jpg
Here's picture of the renowned Fiona Shaw playing Medea.

13060621R00032

Printed in Great Britain
by Amazon.co.uk, Ltd.,
Marston Gate.